Life Is a Love Story

Art and Affirmations

Katie King

ISBN 979-8-88616-565-4 (paperback)
ISBN 979-8-88616-566-1 (digital)

Christian Faith Publishing
832 Park Avenue
Meadville, PA 16335
www.christianfaithpublishing.com

Photo Art done by Les Roholt

Printed in the United States of America

Introduction

Positive affirmations are a wonderful way to change your thinking. I am statements can help you change your core beliefs.

Photo art by Les Roholt

Affirmations by Katie King

Acknowledgment

Thanks to Les for the blessings of the latest art form—photo art.

I am blessed with joyful inspiration.

I am blessed with a beautiful

Ingenious attitude.

I am magical.

God bless the world with hope.

I am a beautiful child of God.

I am empowered by my God.

I am blessed with

an extraordinary mind.

I am filled with an attitude of care.

I am grateful for my life.

I am honored and brave.

Fear is excitement

without the breath.

—Author Gay Hendricks

I deserved to be loved.

God bless the earth.

I am blessed with peaceful contentment.

I cherish God.

God bless the

universe.

I am perfect just as I am.

I am blissful, I am successful,

I am valuable.

Author, Joel Osteen

I feel whole,

Nothing but goodness comes to me.

I adore my feelings of compassion.

I am beautiful on the inside.

Breathing is magical.

God adores me.

I am always loved and respected.

I am calm, I breathe easy.

I see beauty all around me.

Love is ageless.

I am fulfilled with unconditional love.

I am kind-minded.

I am fun to be around;

It is a blessing to know me.

I love my life.

I am healthy and strong.

I am loveable.

Human beings are a thing of wonder.

I am blessed with a loving mind.

I am excited to be alive.

Breathing is fun.

I treasure myself.

I am peaceful.

I am carefree.

God is my soul support.

I love my heart with all of my soul.

My perfect health is loving energy.

I bring joy to God.

I love to be creative.

I am gifted.

Love is healthy energy.

I am free of negative beliefs.

My heart is extraordinary

physically and spiritually.

I love my body.

I am filled with laughter.

I am worthy of wealth.

I am blessed with a bright future.

Wealth is healthy energy,

I am empowered with wealth,

I deserve to be wealthy.

I am appreciated.

I deserve gratitude.

God is my best friend.

God is my hero.

I am spectacular to God.

I bring comfort to the world.

I love my brain.

I am extraordinary.

I am very kind to myself,

I am admired,

I am blessed with ingenuous

thoughts, and ideas.

I am a genius.

I am filled with confidence.

God is life.

I am loved.

God is the wonder of the world.

I adore my feelings.

Money soothes me.

I am fearless.

I am filled with loving joy.

I am deeply in love with God.

I am grateful for God.

I appreciate my life.

Life is phenomenal.

I am blessed with joyful memories.

I feel fabulous.

I am precious.

I cherish God.

I have an awesome smile.

I love my heart.

It is a blessing to be alive.

My life is perfect in every way.

I adore my fear.

I am mindful of my perfect health.

I feel love in my heart.

I am at peace with my past.

I feel at home with myself.

—Author George Leanard

I bring joy to everyone

I know and meet.

I cherish life.

Every day is a fairytale.

Author, Unknown

Living is a miracle.

I am empowered with love.

My heart is beautiful.

I love to learn.

I think great inspiring thoughts.

I am blessed with good fortune.

I beam with Joy.

I love and adore my family.

Love is the heart of the soul.

I am brilliant.

I love to play.

I love to laugh.

I am filled with delight.

I am always loving

And caring to others.

I am worthy of God's love.

I am free.

This is the most treasured

Time of my life.

What a blessing it is to be me!

And now my mind is filled

With positive thoughts!

About the Author

Katie is a retired teacher. Writing is her hobby, and she plans on publishing children's books in the near future. Katie loves the outdoors especially the winter months, and she resides in Minnesota.

Les Roholt is a photographer, artist, and graphic designer.

From 2006 through 2010, he was the art director for the Minneapolis-based Sentinel magazine.

He is a former member of NAPP (National Association of Photoshop Professionals).

Most of the images in this book are from Arches National Park. The entrance is located about one mile from Moab, Utah. Once you go there you'll never want to leave.

Katie and Les hope you enjoyed the images paired with the profound affirmations. If so, let them know.

Les's Email: Les@LesPhotoArt.com

Les's website: Lesphotoart.com

Katie's email: Kingkatie696@gmail.com

www.ingramcontent.com/pod-product-compliance
Lightning Source LLC
Chambersburg PA
CBHW041651150726
48005CB00013BA/1611